ZER
WASTE

Christmas

CRAFTY IDEAS FOR A
SUSTAINABLE CHRISTMAS

CHRISTINE LEECH
& EMMA FRIEDLANDER-COLLINS

DAVID & CHARLES

www.davidandcharles.com

Contents

Reclaim Christmas

The heart of Christmas for us is about spending time with the people we love and celebrating the season. We all have such busy lives that it can feel easier to buy things to make our homes look and feel festive. But we think there is a better way...

This book is all about using the materials around you to bring festive cheer to your home, whether you're celebrating Christmas, Hanukkah, the winter solstice or just looking for some cosy crafts to add a bit of hygge. It's about sitting down to make things and create memories because something you have made yourself has an emotional durability that can't be bought. This connection means we cherish objects for longer and they are much less likely to end up in landfill in a couple of year's time.

We hope you love making the projects in this book as much as we did creating them. Remember to be inspired by your waste and recycling bins. If you don't have exactly the same packaging or materials that we have used, then think outside the box (sometimes literally) and find your own solutions. You may also find you'll need to adjust the sizes and quantities suggested to suit your particular interpretation. Just go for it and have fun.

As much as possible we've made these projects ethical and sustainable. We know it's not perfect! We're on our own sustainability journeys too. All we really want is for you to see the creative opportunities in the things you already have, develop your crafting skills and enjoy making something that you love.

Christine   Emma
x

Tools and Materials

The basis of zero waste crafting is to reuse things that you have around you, so most of these projects can be made from things that you can find in your home. Once you've sourced your materials it's just a case of having a few basic tools and you're good to go.

MATERIALS

Fabric

Lots of the fabrics for these projects come from clothes. With 80% of clothes in second-hand stores ending up in landfill, it's much better to cut them up and turn them into a Christmas stocking or a festive wreath than leave them hanging in a shop. But all of the projects in this book are about rethinking what existing objects are and what new life they can have with some simple transformations, so don't be afraid to get the scissors out.

Plastics and packaging

Make sure you clean out things like milk bottles thoroughly and then leave them somewhere to dry properly. The last thing you want is old milk going everywhere when you start cutting them up.

Silvered packaging

Our greatest discovery for this book was how versatile the silvery insides of crisp (chips) packets could be – if you thought that zero waste means zero sparkle, you'd be wrong! Also look out for silver and gold card from the packaging of treats like smoked salmon or charcuterie meats.

Paints

We always debate about using spray paint, but if it will transform items destined for landfill, we say it's ok! Montana MTN Water Based 300 is a water-based spray paint with minimal environmental impact. Remember to check local council rules but you should be able to put an empty can in the recycling bin. Alternatively, mix acrylic paint with a little PVA glue to help its adhesion to plastics and metal surfaces.

OTHER TOOLS

Bradawl

This is an incredibly useful little tool designed specifically for making holes in things. Bradawls can be bought from DIY or craft stores and are inexpensive.

Glue gun

A glue gun is one of the best purchases any crafter can make. It's easy to use and can glue everything from fabric to plastics and metals with no strong toxic smells. Beware the gun tip and glue as they can get very hot!

Pinking shears

These are scissors that add a decorative edge to fabric and can also help prevent fraying.

Skandi

This clean but cosy look lends itself perfectly to a less commercial Christmas, so add some 'hygge' without the hype to your zero waste festivities.

Minimal wreath

This is a great way to make use of things that you already have at home, and when you're done you can just take it apart and pop it back in the cupboard.

Marking out the house. Open out the cardboard box and on the wrong side draw out the fronts, sides and roof of the house with the marker pen. You can either use the template (*see Templates*) or try drawing your own. Cut out and glue together **(1)**.

Make the snow. Use scissors to cut a patch of towel to make some 'snow' for the house to stand on. The towel will fray and there will be lots of little bits of cotton. Keep these and use them as decorative snow **(2)**.

Hang the wreath. Cut a length of string to approximately 30cm (12in) long, feed it through the opening mechanism on the edge of the cake tin and tie the ends together. Hang it up in the desired location **(3)**.

Assembling the scene. Place the 'snow' patch in the bottom of the tin, put the cardboard house on it and arrange the pine cones and sprigs of greenery around it. Sprinkle with the loose bits of cotton to finish **(4)**.

You will need

- Cardboard box
- Spring form cake tin
- Old white towel
- Pine cones and sprigs of fir or pine
- Scissors/craft knife
- Marker pen and ruler
- Glue
- String

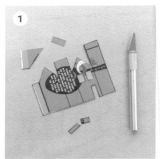

Dala Treat Horse

These little horses make perfect place cards and are a great alternative to crackers, just write each guest's name on their saddles and fill their hollow bodies with treats.

"If you give everyone a paper placemat you can have lots of fun round the dinner table using the horses' pencil legs for doodling, drawing and writing your own Christmas jokes."

You will need

- Toilet roll
- Plain paper
- Bradawl
- Four pencils
- Secateurs or junior hacksaw
- White card from a packaging box
- Tissue paper
- Scissors
- Pens
- Glue stick

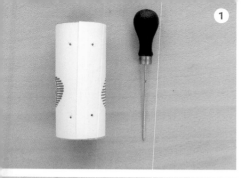

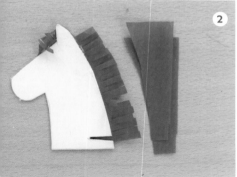

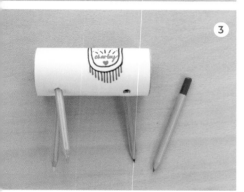

Cover the body. Use the toilet roll as a template and cut a piece of white paper the same length and circumference as it. Draw a saddle on the paper, add a name if you'd like to use the horse as a place setting, and glue in place around the toilet roll. Use a bradawl to make four holes underneath for the pencil legs to fit into **(1)**.

Make the head. Fold the card in half. Draw a horse's head so that the nose touches the fold in the card, and cut it out. Make a 2cm (¾in) slot in the bottom and cut a corresponding slot in the body of the horse so they fit together. Open up the folded head and glue two pieces of tissue paper on the inside, positioning them along the neck and in front of the ear, fold closed and glue together. Trim the tissue paper into the shape of a mane **(2)**.

Make the legs. Trim the four pencils so they are all the same length, using a junior hacksaw, a pair of garden secateurs or even just a bread knife. Next sharpen them to a point and use the pointed end to widen the holes in the body. Insert the legs **(3)**.

Make the tail. Cut a piece of tissue paper 30 x 30cm (12 x 12in). Fold it in half and make a cut every 5mm (¼in) all the way up the open edge, cutting in to half the width of the tissue paper, to make the tail. Add the head to the horse, then pop your table treats inside, roll up and twist the tail in place and insert into the body of the horse **(4)**.

Festive Cross Stitch Jumper

A stocking stitch jumper makes the perfect grid for cross stitching on. Here's how to create a simple but striking skandi design.

Stitching in the jumper. To use the knit as a grid think of the 'outty' stitches as the holes and ignore the 'inny' stitches. Work into every other row to create a square. To start, insert the needle from the back through the middle of a knit stitch, this will be the bottom left corner **(1)**. Skip a row and insert the needle into the next knit stitch to the right **(2)**. (*See also Techniques: Stitches.*)

Start the design. To create this design measure down 20cm (8in) from the top of the shoulder and make a row of cross stitches across the front of the jumper. It's easiest to start with a straight line like this as it helps keep the rest of your stitches nice and even **(3)**.

Follow the charted motifs. Use the motifs in the cross stitch chart (*see Templates*) to create your own winter scene. Different jumpers will be different sizes so add as many or as few trees and houses as you like.

Create the fairy lights. Using a little coloured yarn (leftover bits are great for this), insert your needle from the back and go around the knit stitch a couple of times then tie off at the back **(4)**.

You will need

- Yarn needle
- Yarn
- Scissors
- Knitted jumper

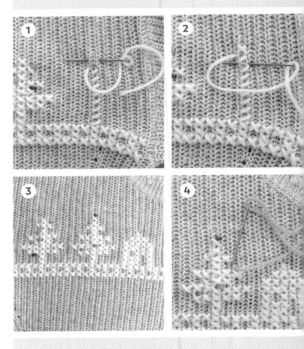

"Once the season is over it's easy to snip off the decorative yarn, and have all the fun of coming up with a different design next year."

Berry Wrap

Decorative paper is much harder to recycle, so we've come up with ways to make natural plant-based paint that is completely recyclable.

Make the red paint. We gathered blackberries at the end of the summer and stored them in the freezer, but you can use any red berries. Press the berries through a sieve with a teaspoon and collect the juice in a bowl **(1)**.

Make the green paint. We had a little winter spinach left in the garden, but you can use any dark green leaves. Place them in a pestle and mortar with a tiny splash of boiling water and grind to a paste **(2)**.

Paint a berry pattern. Take a paint brush and use the red/purple paint to make a cluster of three dots, then use the green paint to paint a few little lines coming away from them for the leaves. You can of course create your own design, feel free to experiment! **(3)**

Wrap with string. We want to avoid sticky tape when wrapping presents, so tying them with twine is an elegant and sustainable way to secure your wrapped gift **(4)**. Finish it off by adding some foliage.

You will need

- Plain paper
- Berries
- Spinach
- Teaspoon
- Sieve
- Paintbrush
- Ceramic bowls
- Pestle and mortar

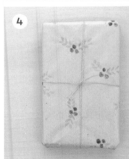

"You can use anything from petals to salad leaves to make your paint, and usually you only need a tiny bit of water to get the juices flowing!"

Advent village

Creating a little advent village in the corner of your home, gently lit with fairy lights and complete with mini trees, is a great way to evoke a festive feeling.

"This village uses old drinks cartons, which have their chimneys already in place, but you can use any packaging. We've used a tin of old wood paint for this, as it gives great coverage and uses up something that was going to waste. "

You will need

- Empty cartons
- 2 tbsp flour
- 2 tbsp water
- Small sponge or old rag
- Old paint
- Paintbrush
- Craft knife
- Ruler
- Pencil
- Salt dough (see Techniques: Salt Dough)
- Evergreen twigs and berries

Prepare the cartons. Wash the cartons thoroughly and make sure they are dry. Use the pencil and ruler to measure out the windows and doors and then use a craft knife to cut them out **(1)**. The key to creating a cohesive design is to make all the windows and doors the same shape and size. It will create a rhythm across your little houses, just like in a real street. On the back of the carton cut a hole large enough to tuck a little advent gift into, and to pop some fairy lights in if you like.

Decorate the cartons. Mix together the flour and water and use the sponge to lightly dab it on to the surface of the carton, this will create a sandy, stony texture on the surface and help the paint to stick better. Once the flour and water mix is dry, paint the house – you may need a few coats **(2)**.

Make the tree stands. Make a salt dough using half the quantities given in the recipe in the Techniques section (*see Techniques: Salt Dough*) and roll out a nice chunky sausage shape. Cut it into pieces, gently roll into balls and then use a pencil or paintbrush to create a hole in the middle **(3)**. Allow to dry naturally for a few days or pop in the oven on a low heat for three hours. Once dry pop in a little spring of evergreen foliage to make a tree **(4)**.

Assemble the village. Add numbers from 1 to 25 on your village buildings – some can be apartments! – and arrange with the trees. Then place a gift inside each building. You could get even more creative by threading fairy lights throughout the village or adding some fake snow. Make your village as ornate or simple as you like. It's Christmas after all!

Solstice Garland

This garland celebrates the spirit of the season by using beautiful imprints of found flora to decorate salt dough stars.

You will need

- Salt dough
- Star pastry cutter
- Rolling pin
- Greaseproof (wax) paper
- Knitting needle or pointy tool
- Thin twine
- Suitable size branch/stick

Roll out the dough. Make the salt dough (*see Techniques: Salt Dough*) then on a piece of greaseproof paper, roll it out until it's about 5mm (¼in) thick **(1)**.

Create the imprints. Place your twig or leaf on the dough and then firmly but gently roll across with the rolling pin. Carefully peel the twig or leaf away **(2)**.

Make the stars. Still working on the greaseproof paper cut out the stars using the pastry cutter **(3)**. Use the knitting needle to make a hole at the top point and bottom middle of each star. Peel the excess dough away, carefully move the stars to a baking sheet and put them in the oven for three hours on a low heat, or pop them on a warm window sill for a few days.

Hang the garland. Cut a 75cm (29½in) length of twine, tie one end around the stick and thread the other end through the top hole of a star. Tie as many stars along the stick as you like, on different lengths of twine. To create more depth to the garland use the holes at the bottom middle of the stars to hang extra stars **(4)**. Use a piece of twine to hang the garland on the wall.

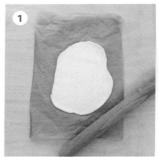

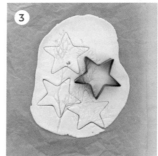

"If you don't have a bit of green space nearby to forage for twigs and leaves you can use anything from lace to Lego men to create different designs."

Hot

··

We're aiming for zero waste, not zero fun. Turn up the heat, draw some inspiration from the culture of warmer countries, and add a blaze of colour to your Christmas.

Pompom Jumper

Pompoms are a great way to make a jumper festive, and you can re-use them next year to create other decorations.

Cut out the pompom maker. Cut two 9 x 14cm (3½ x 5½in) rectangles from the corrugated card. One rectangle must have the corrugation running horizontally, and the other vertically. In the centre of each piece cut out a 3 x 10cm (1⅛ x 4in) section as shown. On one piece only glue the lolly sticks along each edge and across the bottom **(1)**.

Assemble the pompom maker. Using the spare card from the cut out sections, make thin strips and glue next to the sticks. Make sure the strips have the corrugation going in opposite directions – this is what will give it strength. Then glue the other piece on top to finish **(2)**.

Make the pompoms. Using any colour and weight yarn you like, wrap around the pompom maker until you have a good, thick amount. Cut a short length of yarn, tie tightly around the middle and pull off the card **(3)**.

Finish and attach. Cut all the loops **(4)** and trim until the yarn is all the same length and you have a lovely, fluffy pompom. Using a yarn needle, insert through the jumper, up through the centre of the pompom and then back through the jumper. Tie off tightly to secure.

You will need

- Corrugated card
- 3 lolly sticks
- Glue gun
- Yarn and yarn needle
- Scissors

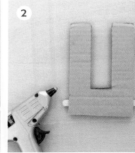

"When it's all over you can take the pompoms off and use them to make a garland, decorate a crown or just cuddle those fluffy balls of joyfulness."

Fabric Flower Wreath

Use up fabric from your stash, or if you have a favourite shirt or jumper that you can't bear to get rid of, repurpose it into flowers for this beautiful heirloom wreath.

Prepare the fabrics. Make a mixture that is equal parts PVA glue and water. Lay all your fabrics on top of each other on a large protected surface. Paint each one on both sides with the PVA mixture. Once you have painted one, hang it to dry somewhere, but try to keep the fabric as flat as possible. I find drying outside is ideal, then finished off on the radiator overnight. By working with the fabrics in a stack, the last one is usually already soaked in PVA mixture by the time you get to it.

Make the leaves. Using the templates (*see Templates*) cut a selection of holly and ivy leaves. To make them look more 3D, pinch the leaves down their centre point and add a little glue to the stalk to secure. Curl the leaves by dragging the closed blades of a pair of scissors along their edges **(1)**.

Make the anemone petals. Cut a circle from your fabric and fold in quarters. Holding the folded centre in one hand, cut a heart shape through the four layers of fabric **(2)**, then snip the tip from the centre and open out.

You will need

- Selection of thin fabrics – cottons, silks, denim, corduroy, velvet
- Old jumper or knitted fabric
- PVA glue
- Old container and large paintbrush
- Cardboard box
- Dinner plate and smaller side plate
- Scissors or craft knife
- Needle and strong thread
- Glue gun

"Look for patterned fabrics that lend themselves to flowers and leaves. The black and white fabric used here is an old shirt from a charity shop – the design lent itself perfectly to being turned into anemones."

Add the anemone centres. Cut and fringe a 3 x 10cm (1¼ x 4in) rectangle of contrasting fabric for the flower stamens. Roll up and then insert into one of the flowers **(3)**. Secure in place with a small dab of glue from your glue gun. As the glue dries pinch the flower around the stamens to improve the shape.

Make the poinsettia. Cut two rectangles from your chosen poinsettia fabric, one 10 x 30cm (4 x 12in) and one 7 x 20cm (2¾ x 8in). Concertina both into five sections **(4)**.

Make the small poinsettia petals. Use the template (*see Templates*) to cut five large and five small petals from each of the folded pieces of fabric. At the base of each petal fold the sides inwards to begin making the petal 3D **(5)**, then curl the tips of the petals with the scissors as before.

Create the centre of the poinsettia. Tie a 3 x13cm (1¼ x 5in) rectangle of fabric in a knot. Gather and twist the ends of the knot together to create texture **(6)**. Basically you just want to make a textured ball of fabric to which you can fix the petals.

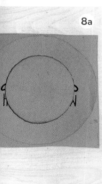

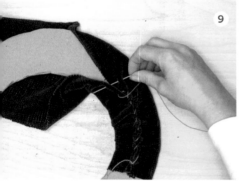

Assemble the poinsettia. Glue each small petal to the back of the fabric ball in a star shape with each one equidistant from the next **(7)**. While the glue is still warm, squish the petals together to make them curl around the flower centre. Glue the larger petals in a similar fashion but offset so they appear between the smaller petals. Curl any petals or leaves that look a bit droopy.

Make the base ring. On the cardboard, draw around a large dinner plate, then centre a smaller side plate in the circle and draw round that. Cut out and use the resulting ring as a template to cut a second ring **(8a)**. Place the two rings together so that the corrugation of one runs 90 degrees to the other to make the base stronger. Glue them together.

Cover the ring in fabric. Measure the circumference of the whole ring to determine the length of the fabric you need, then measure the circumference of one section **(8b)** to determine the width. Add 1cm (½in) to this second measurement and then cut a rectangle from your wreath-covering fabric. Wrap it around the base ring, Use an overstitch to draw the two edges together on the reverse **(9)**. Don't worry about being too neat, a bit of texture looks great.

Add the flowers. Before you glue anything, experiment with positioning the flowers and leaves on the base ring in different compositions. When you are happy with the design, secure each flower and leaf in place with the glue gun **(10)**.

Piñatica Table Favours

These table favours make a sweet alternative to crackers. Fill them with a hat and the usual terrible joke, but maybe find a more thoughtful gift for each guest.

"These piñatica look great sitting on a plate on your Christmas table but also work well as hanging ornaments with the addition of a little ribbon or cord to the top."

You will need

- Thin card – silver-lined milk cartons work really well
- Covering materials – a selection of old gift wrap, colourful plastic postage bags and silver-lined crisp (chips) packets
- Craft knife and cutting mat
- Pinking shears
- Scissors
- Glue stick or double-sided tape
- Split pin paper fasteners.
- Large needle or bradawl
- Thin gold yarn or embroidery floss

Cut out the basic shape. Enlarge the template (*see Templates*) and cut out. Fix to the cardboard then cut out using a craft knife and cutting mat. Alternatively you can draw round the template and then cut out with scissors **(1)**.

Score the folds. Use the back of a pair of scissors and a ruler to score each side of the diamond **(2)**.

Construct the diamond. Glue or fix a strip of double-sided tape along the uppermost side of each tab and fold the card up to create a diamond-shaped piñatica. The tabs will stick to the inside of the piñatica **(3)**.

Prepare the coverings. Use pinking shears to cut 4cm (1½in) wide strips from the length of your covering materials, then use straight scissors to fringe them half-way – use the zigzags of the pinking sheared edge to ensure your fringe is even **(4)**.

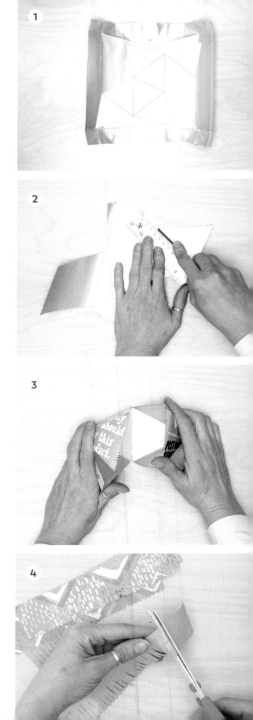

Cover the piñatica. Cut four 14cm (5½in) wide strips with normal scissors. Use these to cover the piñatica around each open edge **(5)**. First glue a strip to the front and back of the top half, folding the strips round the sides. Trim away the excess then use another piece to cover the other two sides. Repeat with the lower half.

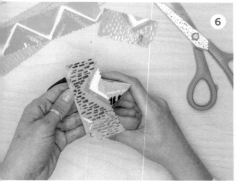

Attach the fringed strips. Fix the first fringed strip to the front of the piñatica. Glue it in place about 5mm (¼in) up from the edge **(6)**. Fix it so there is about a 2cm (¾in) overlap each side, glue down and trim away any excess. Repeat on the back. Fix another strip in place about 1cm (½in) above the previous strip, continue wrapping and trimming each one as you work your way up the piñatica. The two side panels will currently look a little scrappy.

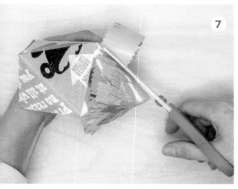

Cover the side panels. When you have covered the front and back, fix corresponding coloured strips in place on the two side panels, carefully trimming away the excess so they look as neat as possible **(7)**. Use the same process for the rest of the piñatica. Cover the very top with an unfringed strip. Cut the edge with pinking shears but don't fringe it. Repeat with the lower half.

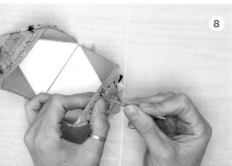

Attach the yarn. Find the centre of the front of the piñatica and make a hole with the needle or bradawl. Insert a split pin and then repeat with the lower half. Wind a piece of thin yarn around the two pins in a figure of eight to keep the piñatica closed **(8)**.

Festive Floral Votives

These floral votive tealights are made from plastic bottles, cut out and carefully melted over a candle to create delicate petal shapes.

"In Colombia they have a festival called Día de las Velitas (Day of the Little Candles) on the 7th December to honour the Virgin Mary. On this day the streets are filled with little candles in decorative votives, and transformed into a magical wonderland. These votives are inspired by that festival."

You will need

- Selection of clean plastic bottles, labels removed
- Scissors
- Water-based spray paints
- Candle
- LED tealights

Prepare the plastic. Cut the neck from a bottle, then cut roughly in half **(1)**.

Trim the edge. Beginning with the shoulder part of the bottle cut six equidistant downward slices. Curve the top of each section to make them look more petal-like **(2)**.

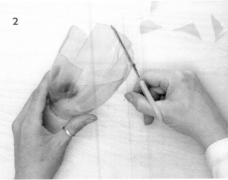

Soften the petals. Light the candle and with extreme care hold the tip of each petal over the flame **(3)**. Begin by holding the bottle quite far from the flame and then gradually move it closer, you will find a point where the plastic starts to soften and curl. You do not want the plastic to start bubbling or go smoky. Beware, the petals may be hot! Do not touch until they have cooled down. Be careful not to burn your fingers!

Shape the petals. Make the petals bend outwards by holding the flower base and one petal tip, hold over the candle at the point where the downward cuts end. As the plastic warms up, bend the petal outwards and hold **(4)**. Remove from the candle and hold till the plastic sets into its new shape. This can all happen in a matter of seconds so be aware!

Make variations. Using the bottom half of the bottle, experiment with cutting different numbers of petals with different shapes. Create flower centres by fringing sections of bottles and softening just the tips so they curl.

Trim the base. Cut the bottom of the flower so it will sit over a LED tealight **(5)**.

Add spray paint. These flowers can look beautiful uncoloured, especially if you have a selection of blue, green and clear bottles to begin with, but they also look great painted. We've use spray paint to get different textures and colours, but acrylic mixed with glue will also adhere to the plastic **(6)**. Always use spray paint in a well ventilated space, and wear a safety mask.

Insert a light. Mix and match your flowers and flower centres to create magical undiscovered floral species. Finally place an LED tealight in the centre of each flower **(7)** and display somewhere they will be appreciated from above.

SAFETY NOTE: DO NOT USE REAL CANDLES TO LIGHT THESE VOTIVES!

"Use a selection of different flowers as a table centre or even place some along a hallway floor or staircase."

Advent Train

This is classic crafting and a great activity for all the family. Getting the kids involved in creating their own advent calendar is a lovely way to lead into the festive season.

"Painting everything before you assemble it gives a much better, more 'professional' finish."

You will need

- 13 toilet rolls
- Cereal box
- Glue gun
- Paints
- Paintbrushes
- Metallic pens
- Marker pens

Make the train carriages and engine. Cut a toilet roll in half, this will make two carriages. Paint with whatever pattern you like **(1)**. For the engine use a whole toilet roll and make six wheels instead of four.

Make the wheels. Paint a strip of cereal box black on both sides and let it dry. Draw around a bottle top as a template, add some spokes with a metallic pen **(2)**, cut out and glue to the carriage.

Add an animal. Fold the card from a cereal box in half and glue together. Trace or draw an animal onto the card using the templates (*see Templates*), or just get creative yourself. Paint in the colour of your animal and allow it to dry. Cut out and add details using marker pens **(3)**.

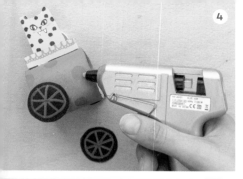

Assemble the animal carriage. Paint and decorate an extra strip of card to keep the animal safe in his carriage, then use the glue gun to secure all the elements in place **(4)**. Add an advent number using metallic pen.

Choose your treats. You can fill your carriages with anything that you like. Fudge wrapped in strips of tissue paper works well as it keeps brilliantly and often comes in paper packaging. You can also find lots of little toys and surprises from second-hand stores **(5)** – once these have been opened and enjoyed, they can be stashed away for next year.

Assemble and fill the carriages. Simply wrap each little object in a bit of tissue paper and secure with a little bit of twine **(6)**. Your train will be quite long when you've finished, but you can get creative in its placement: running along each shelf of a bookcase, circling it around the base of the tree or driving across a mantlepiece.

Favourite PJs Tree Decorations

This little upcycle is a great way to make a memento from your worn out (or grown out of) favourite Christmas pyjamas.

Cut out the picture. Roughly cut out your chosen motif and cut a piece of heat transfer paper the same size and shape. Iron together following the instructions that came with the transfer paper **(1)**.

Cut out the rest. Carefully cut around the print, peel off the backing and iron onto the non-stretchy backing material (we used an old fleece jumper), following the instructions on the paper **(2)**. Once transferred cut out leaving a 1cm (½in) border, and cut out an identical shaped piece to use for the back.

Stitch around the edge. Place the two pieces on top of each other and using a needle and thread sew together leaving a gap to stuff the decoration with. As you are sewing, fold the ribbon over and insert the ends into the top of the decoration to make the hanging loop **(3)**.

Stuff the decoration. You can use shop bought stuffing if you like but we have cut up leftover fabric scraps into little strips and used those to stuff the decorations **(4)**. If you do it in small amounts it's super easy and leaves no waste. Once you have stuffed the decoration you can sew up the final gap in the seam.

You will need

- Old pyjamas with a festive print
- Non-stretchy backing material
- Small strip of ribbon
- Heat transfer paper and iron
- Needle and thread
- Stuffing

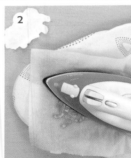

"If you don't want to start cutting up your clothes you can find plenty of festive things in second-hand shops that would love a new life."

Frosty

·····································

It's surprising how sparkly some packaging can be! Pair silvered plastics and card with fairy lights to add a frosty twinkle to your decorations.

Crisp-mas Trees

This festive forest is a great use for silvery crisp packets. Surround with tealights and watch the branches twinkle.

Make the basic cone. Begin by cutting a 20cm (8in) square from the cardboard then roll it up into a cone shape. Secure with glue or double-sided tape. Trim the base of the card so the cone stands up **(1)**.

Wrap the cone. Measure the circumference of the base of your cone and add 2cm (¾in). Cut a rectangle of crisp packet 5cm (2in) tall x that figure. Wrap it around the base of the cone and secure in place **(2)**.

Add the fringed strips. Cut strips of the crisp packet using pinking shears, each about 4.5cm (1¾in) tall. Use scissors to fringe the strips to about halfway, following the pinking sheared edge to keep the fringing even. Using double-sided tape, wrap the first fringe around the cone about 5mm (¼in) from the base **(3)**. Continue wrapping fringed sections around the cone, overlapping them so none of the cardboard is visible.

Finish the tree top. Cut a small semicircle of crisp packet using pinking shears for the curved edge. Add double-sided tape and wrap it around the top of the tree **(4)**. Trim away any excess, then add circles or star shapes, cut from the silver card, to the tree top.

You will need

- Silver lined packaging – crisp (chip) packets
- Food carton cardboard – cereal boxes
- Narrow double-sided tape or a glue stick
- Scissors and pinking shears
- Silver or gold backed card – smoked salmon or dried meats packaging

"You can make your trees all different sizes depending on how tightly or loosely you roll your initial cone. For the tree top star, use a pencil to slightly emboss the card to create patterns.."

Mercury Glass Bottles

This method of creating shimmering glass mimics a traditional technique, but without the dangerous silver mercury – much easier to achieve at home!

Prepare the bottles. Remove any labels and make sure the bottles are clean and dry. Mask off the sections you want to remain free from paint **(1)**.

Apply the diluted vinegar. Mix a solution that is 50% vinegar and 50% water, use about half a cup of each. Place into the spray bottle. Gently mist the bottle on the untaped sides. Try to keep the bottle flat so there aren't too many drips **(2)**.

Spray with gold paint. In a well ventilated space, and wearing a safety mask, cover the water droplets on the bottle with the spray paint **(3)**.

Remove the masking tape. Leave for about 10 seconds and then very gently dab off the paint with the kitchen roll or cloth **(4)**. Leave to dry then peel away the masking tape.

You will need

- 50 / 50 vinegar/water mix in a spray bottle
- Selection of small glass bottles
- Masking tape
- Gold spray paint
- Kitchen roll or old cloth

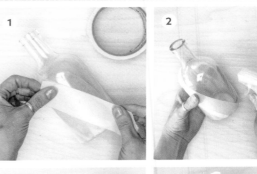

"We have found with practice that gently pressing the cloth over a larger area works much better than dabbing individual droplets, as you get a nicer texture in the paint."

Frosty Fairy Lights

These lights are based on vintage American ones from the 1940s. We love the way the lights sparkle off the tin and make everything even more Christmassy.

"Do you want coloured fairy lights? Use Sharpie pens to colour in each bulb for a bespoke look."

You will need:

- Aluminium tins from takeaways
- Old scissors – the tins will blunt them so don't use your favourites!
- Bradawl
- Empty pen to make indentations in the tin
- String of fairy lights
- Glue gun
- Piece of card
- Large knitting needle

Cut the tin. Trim the sides off a foil tin **(1)**. The edges can be sharp so wear gloves when cutting and polishing for protection.

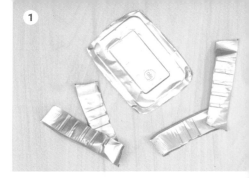

Smooth out the foil. Get rid of any grooves by rubbing with a smooth hard object **(2)**. The lid of a deodorant bottle works well, but anything rounded that is made of firm plastic will work, for example, the base of a shampoo bottle.

Using the templates. Print and cut out the templates (*see Templates*). You don't have to cut them out too neatly as you will be drawing over the design rather than around it onto the tin. Use the empty pen to trace the shapes onto the tin. Using scissors, carefully cut the shapes out, again using gloves to protect your hands **(3)**.

Punch the holes. Place the tin shape onto the piece of cardboard. Use the bradawl to make small holes to form a pattern that will allow the light to shine through **(4)**.

Emboss a pattern. Use the empty pen to make indentations that will capture the light from the fairy lights **(5)**. Draw leaves, snowflakes and other shapes.

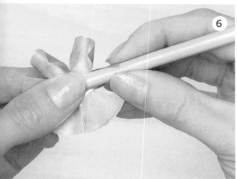

Form the light. Make the centre of the lights by rolling each cut piece around the knitting needle to curl it **(6)**.

Join the pieces. Place the two pieces of tin together and carefully make a hole in the middle of them both using the bradawl **(7)**. Make the hole bigger by inserting a pencil or knitting needle and gradually enlarge it until the shape fits over the fairy light bulb.

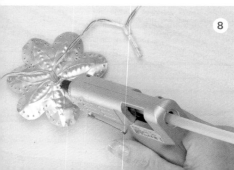

Attaching the lights. The two pieces of tin should be fixed together by the excess tin from the hole being pushed through to the back of the light. Carefully fold this excess tin over to secure. If this doesn't work you can always use a small bit of glue to hold it together. Insert the fairy lights into the hole then fix the two together with a blob of glue on the back of the tin shape **(8)**.

Marbled Jewels

These delicate marbled jewels make great tree decorations or gift tags and it's an ideal way to use up old nail varnishes.

"Every nail varnish seems to behave differently when in contact with water. We've experimented with both cheap and expensive ones from loads of brands and we still can't tell you which works best. They are a law unto themselves!"

You will need

- Frosted or white plastic bottles with flat sides – milk, bleach or laundry detergent bottles
- Pencil
- Scissors
- Old nail varnishes
- A deep plastic tub filled with water
- Cocktail stick (tooth pick) or kebab stick
- Protective gloves
- Hole punch or bradawl
- Cotton or string for hanging

Cut the plastic jewel shapes. Clean and remove any labels from the bottle, then cut them into flat pieces. Using the templates (*see Templates*) trace the jewel shapes on to the plastic and then cut them out. Use a hole punch or bradawl to make a hole at the top. Add a piece of string for a hanging loop **(1)**.

Mix the nail varnishes. Place the container filled with water onto a protected surface. Take a nail varnish and dribble a little on to the water. It may sink to the bottom or disperse, or it may just sit on the surface – any reaction is fine. Add a second colour and then a third **(2)**. The varnishes will react with each other and start to take on a marbled look. Use a cocktail or kebab stick to gently swirl the varnishes together.

Dip the plastic shapes. Take a jewel and keeping it vertical, dip it slowly but confidently into the water and varnish, right to the string, and then pull it out again. You will see the varnish has transferred itself to the plastic. The first one may not be perfect, you may find that there are large globs of varnish or not much varnish at all! Keep experimenting until you have the right combination of varnish swirls and water **(3)**. After a couple of dips, clear the remaining varnish from the top of the water by placing a tissue onto the surface, then have another go.

Hang to dry. Use the string to hang the jewel somewhere to dry. Be careful to cover the floor below as some varnish may drip. You may want to replace the string if it has become clogged with varnish **(4)**.

Celebration Candlesticks

Use these for Hannukah, solstice, Christmas or any holiday you like! Just paint them in colours that suit your decorative scheme.

Make the base. Candlesticks need to be stable, so use the biggest jar lid you have for the base. Make a hole in the centre using a bradawl and widen it with a screwdriver. Fit the chopstick into the hole and make sure it feels secure, but don't glue anything just yet **(1)**.

Make the stem. Make holes with the bradawl in the centres of the bottle tops and fit them on the chopstick interspersed with cotton reels **(2)**. Some of the bottle tops will need to be upside down so there aren't any gaps. Finish with an upside down jar lid.

Secure the candlestick. Mark on the chopstick where the lids come up to, take everything off and use the secateurs to snip the chopstick to the right height **(3)**.

Glue it all in place. Put the lids and reels back on the stick, gluing as you go. The base needs to be weighted for stability, so find something heavy to glue to the underside. A few two pence pieces or big washers work really well **(4)**. Once it's all glued together paint in any colour you like. Wear a mask if you're using spray paint.

You will need

- Bottle tops, cotton reels and two jar lids
- 'Disposable' chopsticks
- Glue gun
- Garden secateurs, bradawl and screwdriver
- 2p pieces/washers
- Acrylic paint/spray paint

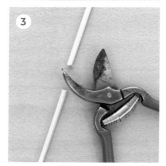

"Any candlestick can fall or be knocked over, but the heavier the base the less chance there is, so for safety's sake weight the bottom, and never leave a lit candle unattended."

Coffee Cup Baubles

Made from things found in The Kitchen Drawer (we've all got one!) artfully glued into little coffee cups, these make for brilliant, one of a kind decorations.

Find your objects. You'll need ribbon to hang the bauble up with, something fluffy or frilly to go at the bottom of the cup, something to be the main feature, and something to make a bow on the handle **(1)**.

Dress the handle. Use a bit of ribbon to tie around the handle to hang the bauble with and then use a scrap of fabric or some thicker ribbon to tie a bow around the top edge of the handle **(2)**.

Fill the cup. Using a glue gun put some spots of glue in place at the bottom and edges of the cup and carefully secure your 'background' material. Scraps of tulle work really well, or a feather, as they create a lovely soft contrast to things like tinsel and beads **(3)**.

Create the main feature. At the front centre of the cup use the glue gun to secure a small bit of tinsel. On top of that glue your 'hero' object with a couple of beads **(4)**.

You will need

- Small coffee cup
- Approximately 20cm (8in) ribbon
- Glue gun
- Bits of tinsel/ribbon/feather
- A 'hero' object – Lego man, trinket, anything!

"Little things that reflect the light work really well once you get them on the Christmas tree among the fairy lights."

Retro

You can re-use and revitalise
some of your favourite memories
of Christmasses gone by with
home-made paper hats and
hand-crafted decorations.

A Christmas Mischief of Mice

Did you know a group of mice is called a mischief? Don't you just want to believe this colourful lot come alive on Christmas Eve and nibble Santa's sherry and mince pie?

"These mice can be used in so many ways. Add a hanging cord and they become tree decorations, have them hold name cards on your table as place settings. Whatever you do, every house should have a Christmas mouse."

You will need

- Odd socks, one per mouse
- Felt for ears
- Paper cotton buds (cotton swab), two per mouse
- Needle and embroidery threads, black for eyes, pink for nose and any colour you like for the front legs
- Scissors
- Sewing machine or needle and thread
- Fabric glue
- Bradawl
- A small amount of toy stuffing and/or small beads or lentils for weight (optional)

Make the mouse tail and body. From a sock, cut a 2.5 x 12cm (1in x 4¾in) rectangle for the tail. Make it look more tail like by stretching the rectangle between your fingers. Take another sock for the body, turn it inside out and lay it flat. Cut a diagonal line across the sock. Start about 5cm (2in) from the sock opening and finish about 10cm (4in) away on the other side **(1)**. Experiment with these measurements to create different sized mice.

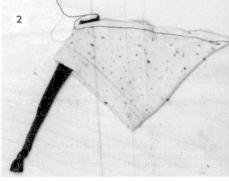

Add the tail. Sandwich the tail between the two body layers as shown, then machine or hand sew with a 5mm (¼in) seam allowance along the diagonal cut line, making sure to sew over the tail to secure it in place **(2)**. Turn the mouse right side out.

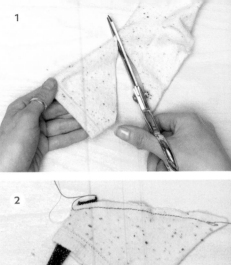

Stuff the mouse. Hand sew a line of running stitches (*see Techniques: Stitches*) around the sock cuff about 5mm (¼in) in from the edge. Fill the mouse with a little toy stuffing in the nose and then stuff the rest with the remaining sock cut into small pieces **(3)**. If you don't have toy stuffing, any little offcuts of soft fabric will work.

Close the bottom. Squish the stuffing around as you are filling the body to make sure you are creating a nice mousey shape. Once full, gather the running stitch and tie a tight double knot. Over stitch the hole with a couple of stitches then secure **(4)**.

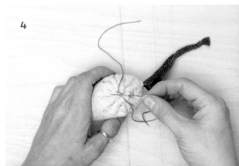

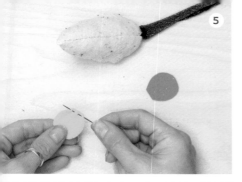

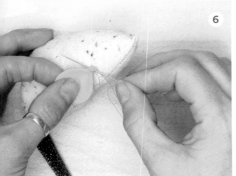

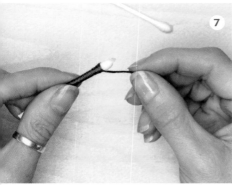

Make the ears. From the felt, cut two slightly oval-shaped circles for ears. Cut the base of each flat. Sew a couple of running stitches along the flat edge **(5)**.

Attach the ears. Tie a tight knot in the cotton to gather the stitches and the base of the ear. Sew the ear to the head. Repeat with the second ear **(6)**.

Embroider the features. Using the pink embroidery thread, sew four or five over stitches at the very tip of the head for the mouse's nose. Sew two French knots for eyes (*see Techniques: Stitches*).

Add the mouse arms. Remove a bud from one end of a cotton bud. Cover the stick and other bud in glue, then carefully wrap with the embroidery thread, till you reach the tip of the bud **(7)**. Cut the thread, and you may need to add extra glue here to secure the end. Repeat with the second arm. Use the bradawl to make a hole the size of the cotton bud in the mouse's body **(8)**. Insert the arm into the hole, glue in place. Bend the arm to create different positions. Repeat with the second arm.

Add extra decorations. You can dress up your mouse by making small paper accessories, such as hats. You'll find that with a little imagination lots of Christmas ornaments can be repurposed for your new mouse family.

Plastic Bag Pompom Wreath

Simple yet effective, this wreath is just a circle of pompom flowers, or snowballs! It'll make a dent in your plastic bag collection, and being waterproof it's also perfect for hanging outside.

"We've used all white bags but ones with patterns or wording can also look great. To avoid the wreath looking too much like 'it's made from plastic bags' limit the mix of colours and take time planning the order of the pompoms."

You will need

- Selection of plastic bags and plastic wrap
- Glue gun
- Wire coathanger
- Small baubles
- Coloured drink bottle lids

Prepare the bags. Take your plastic bags and cut away the handles and bottom of the bags. Cut down one side to open the bag out flat. Layer up four rectangles from different bags. We tend to use two bags per flower and alternate the bags when we stack them. The size of the original bags will determine the size of your flowers. Ideally all your rectangles will be of a similar size. A width of approximately 28cm (11in) works well **(1)**.

Fold the bags. Starting at one of the short ends, concertina the stack up. Make the concertina folds about 2.5cm (1in) wide **(2)**. Keeping the concertina folded, cut in half and set one piece aside. We tend to place it under a heavy object so it doesn't unfold!

Tie the centres. Take one of the bag handles and tie it in a double knot around the concertina. Pull tight to gather the middle slightly **(3)**.

Trim the ends. Cut each end of the concertina into an arc shape **(4)**

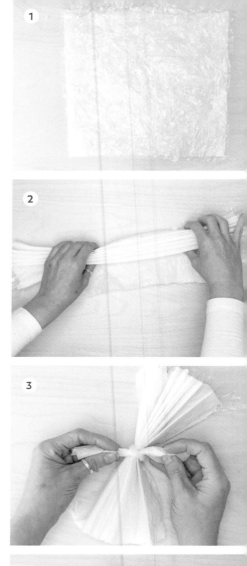

Shape the pompom flowers. Gently fan out each side of the concertina and separate the individual layers, pulling them apart to make a 3D flower shape **(5)**.

Make the wire circle base. Bend the wire coat hanger in to a circle shape **(6)**.

Attach the pompom flowers. Before fixing the flowers to the hanger lay them out to create a pattern that you like. As you have two flowers from each set of bags you can make a nicely symmetrical pattern. Tie each flower to the hanger with a double knot **(7)**. You may not be able to pull the knots too tight but you can secure them further later on.

Fill the hanger with the pompom flowers. Use the glue gun to add a blob of glue either side of each knot **(8)**. This will secure the flowers to the metal wreath more firmly. Finish off by gluing the small baubles and drinks lids into place on the front of the wreath using the glue gun.

Newspaper Hats

We love these hats! If you are looking for a post-lunch activity, why not challenge everyone to follow these instructions and make their own?

Paint the newspaper squares. Paint one side of the newspaper in brightly coloured patterns. Cover the whole of the paper so not much newsprint shows through. Leave to dry.

Make the first folds. With the painted side down, fold the square in half from top to bottom, then in quarters from right to left **(1)**.

Fold the side. Open out then fold the right-hand side in to the middle crease **(2)**.

You will need

- Squares of newspaper (ideally with not too many photographs on), sizes: large head 70cm (27½in), medium 50cm (20in), small 40cm (15¾in)
- Paints and large brushes
- Metallic crisp (chips) packets or similar
- Coloured magazine paper
- Small metallic cupcake cases
- Washi tape
- Glue

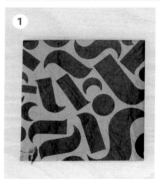
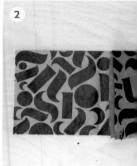

"If origami blows your mind then the simplest party hat to make is a painted square rolled up into a cone shape and secured with glue. Supply hair grips or a piece of elastic fixed to each side of the hat to help the wearer keep it in place."

Fold the corner. Open out then fold the right-hand corner into a triangle to meet the previous crease **(3)**.

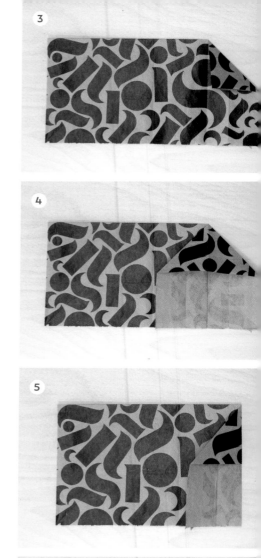

Open the triangle. Take the lower right-hand corner and pull towards the middle crease, opening out the triangle at the top and refolding it so it lies flat **(4)**.

Fold the rest behind. Fold the remaining right-hand piece of paper behind **(5)**.

And now the other side. Repeat steps 2–5 on the left-hand side **(6)**.

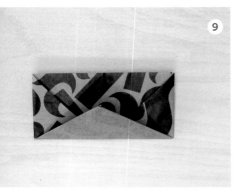

Fold the bottom corners. Fold both bottom corners to form triangles setting at the middle crease **(7)**.

Make the point. Fold the bottom corner triangles upwards to create a point **(8)**.

Make the other point. Repeat steps 7 and 8 on the other side **(9)**.

Open the hat. Open out the base of the crown by pulling it carefully apart. The middle of the crown should sink downwards creating four points **(10)**.

Decorate the crown. Add upright tassels at each point. Make the tassels using strips of magazine papers and crisp packets curled around scissor points. Make each strip about 20cm (8in) long. Place about six strips together and fold in half. Secure with washi tape then glue in place at the tip of each point. Use cupcake cases and coloured paper to make jewels to decorate the crown fronts.

Retro Tree Decorations

Christine says: 'one of my favourite places is Palm Springs – I love the mid-century architecture and the stylish colour combinations. These decorations draw on that style'.

"Although these decorations are inspired by delicate 1950s glass baubles, they are a lot more hardwearing!"

You will need

- Metallic card – base from smoked salmon packaging
- A magazine or double-sided, colourful paper
- Scalpel, ruler and cutting mat
- Silver yarn and needle
- Glue gun
- Old crisp packets with metallic insides
- Bamboo skewer or similar pointed implement
- Hole punch
- Bradawl
- Wire from a bag tie or fuse wire

Prepare the paper and templates. Cut a rectangle of paper 8 x 17cm (3¼ x 6¾in) for the long decoration and another one 9 x 21cm (3½ x 8¼in) for the wide decoration. Trace and cut out the templates (*see Templates*).

Mark the concertina. With the rectangle of paper in a landscape position, score lines at 1 cm (½in) intervals using the back of a pair of scissors, a bamboo skewer or similar pointed implement to score the paper without cutting through it **(1)**.

Create the concertina. Fold the paper up into a fan shape, and then carefully fold in half and glue together **(2)**. Open the fan out into a circle and glue the other edges together **(3)**.

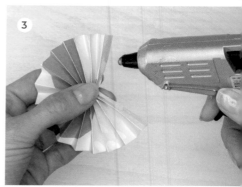

Cut out the templates. Place the template onto the metallic card and tape in place. Cut them out using the scalpel and cutting mat - it's easier to cut a smooth circle if you do it in sections first **(4)**.

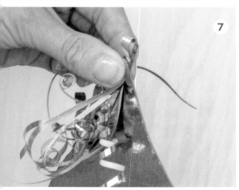

Make the hanging holes. Use the hole punch and bradawl to make holes as shown on the templates. Tie several knots in the silver yarn then thread through the bottom small hole. Thread across the cutaway circle through the second hole, then through the large hole at the top twice – this helps keep the yarn taut across the cutaway circle **(5)**.

Position the fan. Place the fan circle behind the silver yarn so the yarn lays along one of the grooves of the fan. Make sure the fan circle is central to the cutaway circle. Add a small blob of glue above the yarn, then pinch the fan together to secure the yarn in place **(6)**.

Make the tassel. Use scissors or a scalpel and ruler to cut thin strips from the crisp packet. Curl the ends of each strip by pulling them across the back of scissor blades.

Attach the tassel. Gather the strips up and fold them in half, push the folded section through the hole at the base of the decoration, carefully pulling half the ends of the tassel through the hole **(7)**. Fold the tassel over the decoration and then secure the two halves together using the wire **(8)**. Alternatively you could just glue another small piece of crisp packet around the strips to secure.

Jam Jar Advent Calendar

Use your favourite pretty jars to make this advent calendar and when Christmas is over you'll find them super useful for storing all your bits and bobs in too.

Add the toy to the lid. With the lid on the jam jar work out the best place to glue the toy to the lid. Use the glue gun to fix the toy in place **(1)**.

Spray with primer. Keeping each lid and jar separate, coat with the spray primer. Work in a well ventilated space, ideally outdoors, and always wear a mask. Allow the jars and lids to dry **(2)**.

Paint the jars. When the primer is dry coat each jar and lid with the coloured spray paints. Make sure you spray matching jars and lids the same colour. Allow to dry **(3)**.

Add the numbers. When the paint is dry write a different number, from 1 to 24, on each jar **(4)**. Fill each jam jar with a different small gift then decide if you are going to display them all at once or build up your display over the month.

You will need

- 24 jam jars with lids
- 24 small toys or old Christmas ornaments
- Water-based primer spray paint, and spray paints in varying colours
- Permanent marker
- Glue gun

"Be creative with what you hide inside the jars. If you want to gift food and sweets (candy) then make the calendar well in advance to avoid any smells from the spray paint lingering."

Jumper Stocking and Wristwarmers

Upcycling a Christmas jumper into a stocking is a great way to reuse it. Then you can use the sleeves to make a pair of wristwarmers for yourself too.

Cut out and sew the stocking. Using a washable pen, draw the shape of the stocking on the jumper. Use the rib at the bottom as the top edge of the stocking. Using the zigzag stitch on the sewing machine sew around the outline and then use then pinking shears to cut approximately 1cm (½in) from the stitches **(1)**.

Add the ribbon and decoration. Fold the ribbon in half and pin it to the back inside edge of the stocking and stitch in place. You can leave your stocking plain or decorate the front with anything you like **(2)**.

Make a pair of wristwarmers. Turn the sleeves inside out and measure and cut 20cm (8in) from the edge of each sleeve. Cut length ways so that each sleeve is 8cm (3¼in) across and use your hand as a template to work out where you need to make a thumb hole **(3)**.

Cut and sew. Cut out the wristwarmers, leaving an extra bit of seam allowance around the thumb hole. Sew up the edge leaving a gap for the thumb, fold over the thumb seam and stitch in place **(4)**.

You will need

- A jumper
- Washable pen
- Pinking shears
- 30cm (12in) wide ribbon
- Yarn needle

"There are lots of ways to reuse a jumper. Once you get over the fear of cutting into knit you'll start thinking of all sorts of ways to use the material."

Techniques

STITCHES

Here are a couple of embroidery stitches that you can use to decorate all manner of festive makes, and a description of essential running stitch.

Running Stitch

This can be done on a machine or by hand and it is the simplest of stitches: needle goes in, needle comes out a little further along, repeat. And that's it.

Cross Stitch

This stitch is great for creating blocks of embroidered colour, or for stitching smaller motifs. It's explained in detail in the Festive Cross Stitch Jumper project.

How to cross stitch, part 1.
Thread the needle, make a knot in the end, and then insert the needle from the back of the jumper to the front. This will be the bottom left-hand starting point of the cross. Insert the needle back in at a point above and to the right of where you started **(1)**.

Cross stitch, part 2. To complete the cross insert your needle in from the back at the bottom right, opposite your starting point and complete the stitch by inserting the needle into the top left spot **(2)**.

French Knots

Bring your needle up from the back of your fabric then hold it flat on the surface of the fabric and wrap the thread around the needle twice (not too tightly) **(3)**. Gradually pull the needle through the thread loops and slide them down the thread on to the fabric. Insert the needle back into the fabric close to the original stitch **(4)**.

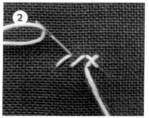

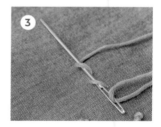

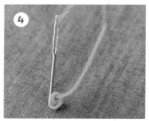

SALT DOUGH

This is a brilliant zero waste material! It uses store cupboard staples, is biodegradable and once dry can last for an exceptionally long time if cared for.

You will need

1 cup of flour

½ cup of salt

½ cup of water

Mixing bowl

To make the dough, mix the flour, salt and water together in a bowl and knead for 10 minutes to make the dough elastic.

Once you have created your salt dough masterpiece you will need to allow it to dry out for several days. You can speed the process up by putting your salt dough creation in an oven on a very low heat for about three hours. It can then be painted or left in its original colour.

Templates

All templates are shown at 50%. You can download full-size versions of these templates from www.davidandcharles.com.

SKANDI

Festive Cross Stitch Jumper cross stitch chart (shown full size)

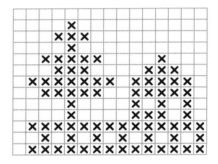

House

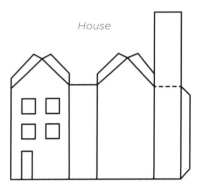

HOT

Fabric Flower Wreath

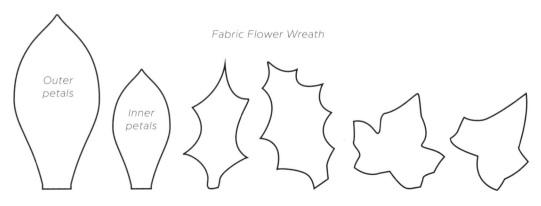

Outer petals

Inner petals

Poinsettia petal

Holly

Ivy

Piñatica Table Favours

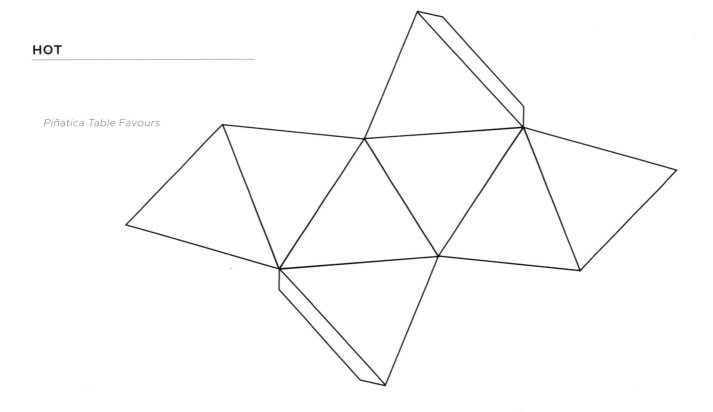

Advent Train

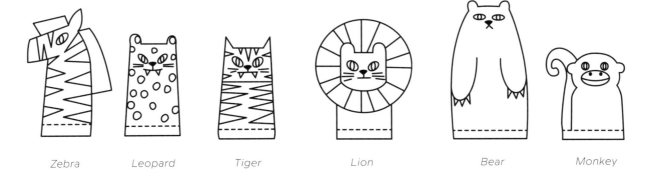

Zebra   Leopard   Tiger   Lion   Bear   Monkey

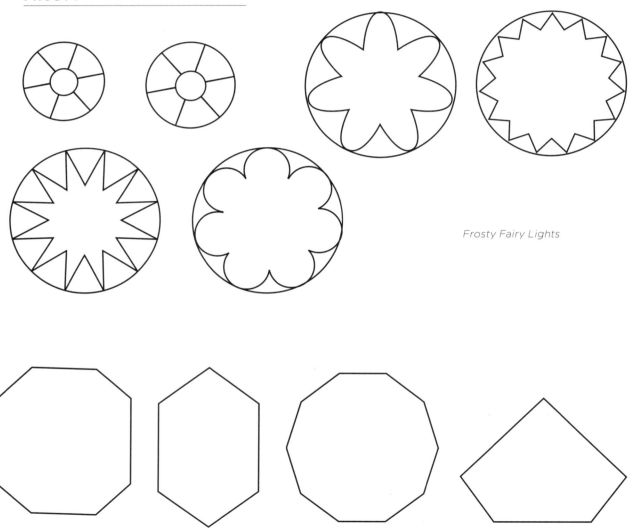

Frosty Fairy Lights

Marbled Jewels

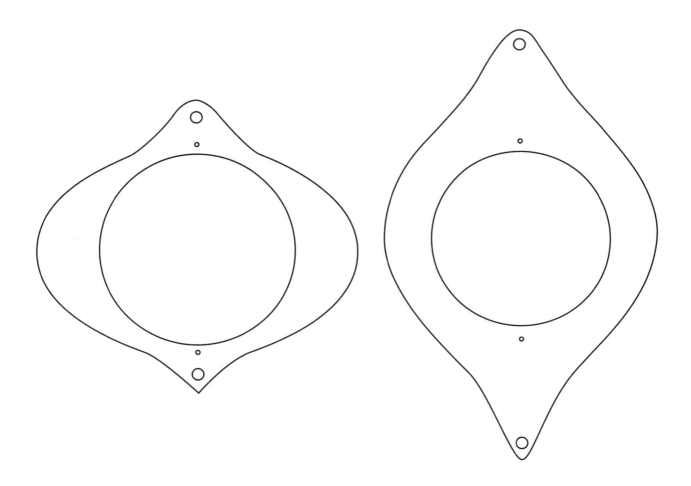

Retro Tree Decoration (wide)   Retro Tree Decoration (long)

Authors

Christine

Christine Leech is an author, designer, maker, stylist, and workshop host. She won her first craft-related award at just 5 years old (best hemmed handkerchief in the village Flower Show). This led to a life filled with cardboard, fabric, scissors and glue.

This is her eleventh book and her third in the Zero Waste Craft series. The first, *Zero Waste Gift Wrap*, is filled with beautiful projects for sustainable wrapping, and the second, written with Emma, offers great ideas for zero waste crafting for the kitchen.

She lives by the adage *'A Creative Mess is Better Than Idle Tidiness'* which gives her the excuse to never tidy up! She documents her crafty life on her Instagram @sewyeah, where she shares daily inspiration, step-by-step projects and videos.

Emma

Emma's first foray into upcycling was at nine years old when she turned her curtains into a Ming the Merciless dressing gown. At 41 she came full circle and got an MA in Sustainable Design (but didn't use her curtains this time).

Over the last 10 years she has written numerous books on crochet, craft and upcycling and is a regular contributor to UK craft mags and websites. She loves teaching and has run workshops all over the country, from The Clothes Show to her children's primary school.

Emma is passionate about sharing ways to transform everyday materials with the power of craft, and lots of these can be found on her Instagram @steelandstitch.

Our thanks to...

We would both like to thank Sara Callard for believing in Zero Waste Living, the role craft can play in making a difference and for commissioning this book. Anna, Jason, Jess, Pru and Jane for making it look beautiful, sound right and feel lovely.

Emma would like to dedicate this book to her twin sister Katie and thank her for all her festive input.

Christine would like to thank everyone who keeps her going on her crafty journey, her family and all the usual suspects. Thanks to lovely Ana, whose Colombian heritage inspired the Festive Floral Votives. Thanks to Helen and Alice – truly excellent new friends and inspirational Craft Gurus – and to Emma, the most wonderful craft-wife a girl can have.

We would both like to thank everyone who buys this book and in doing so moves one step further towards a more sustainable lifestyle and a happier planet.

Index

We have considered the environmental
impact of this book by using soy-based inks,
printing on FSC paper and using unbleached,
uncoated duplex board for the front cover.

Printed in China by Asia Pacific for:
David and Charles, Ltd
Suite A, Tourism House, Pynes Hill, Exeter,
EX2 5WS

10 9 8 7 6 5 4 3 2 1

Senior Commissioning Editor: Sarah Callard

Editor: Jessica Cropper

Project Editor: Jane Trollope

Head of Design: Anna Wade

Senior Designer: Lucy Waldron

Art Direction and Styling:
Prudence Rogers

Book Layout and Design: Anna Wade

Photography: Jason Jenkins,
Christine Leech and
Emma Friedlander-Collins

Pre-press Designer: Ali Stark

Production Manager: Beverley Richardson

David and Charles publishes high-quality
books on a wide range of subjects.
For more information visit
www.davidandcharles.com.

Layout of the digital edition of this book
may vary depending on reader hardware
and display settings.